Somehow, out of all the twists and
turns our lives could have taken, and
out of all the chances we might have
missed, it almost seems like we were
given a meant-to-be moment...

that turned out to mean
the world to me.

To the One Person
I Consider to Be

My Soul Mate

*Loving messages meant to be shared
with a very special person*

by D. Pagels

Blue Mountain Press ™

SPS Studios, Inc., Boulder, Colorado

Library of Congress Catalog Card Number: 00-029682
ISBN: 0-88396-558-5

Certain trademarks are used under license.

Manufactured in the United States of America
Fifth Printing: September 2002

♲ This book is printed on recycled paper.

This book is printed on fine quality, laid embossed, 80 lb. paper. This paper has been specially produced to be acid free (neutral pH) and contains no groundwood or unbleached pulp. It conforms with all the requirements of the American National Standards Institute, Inc., so as to ensure that this book will last and be enjoyed by future generations.

Library of Congress Cataloging-in-Publication Data

Pagels, D., 1950-
    To the one person I consider to be my soul mate : loving messages meant to be shared with a very special person / by D. Pagels.
        p. cm.
    ISBN 0-88396-558-5 (alk. paper)
    1. Love poetry, American. I. Title.

PS3566.A3372 T6 2000
811'.6—dc21

                                                    00-029682
                                                    CIP

SPS Studios, Inc.
P.O. Box 4549, Boulder, Colorado 80306

A Soul Mate Is a
Wondrous Thing

The most wonderful of all things in life, I believe,
is the discovery of another human being with
whom one's relationship has a glowing depth,
beauty, and joy....

This inner progressiveness of love between two
human beings is a most marvelous thing; it cannot
be found by looking for it or by passionately
wishing for it. It is a sort of Divine accident.

— Sir Hugh Walpole

I am so glad that you are a part of
my life. It is such a privilege — to
know you, to share myself with you,
and to walk together on the paths
that take us in so many beautiful
directions.

I had heard of "soul mates"
before, but I never knew
such a person could exist —

until I met you...

Somehow, out of all the twists and turns our lives could have taken, and out of all the chances we might have missed, it almost seems like we were given a meant-to-be moment — to meet, to get to know each other, and to set the stage for a special togetherness.

When I am with you, I know that I am in the presence of someone who makes my life more complete than I ever dreamed it could be...

I turn to you for trust, and you give it openly. I look to you for inspiration, for answers, and for encouragement, and — not only do you never let me down — you lift my spirits up and take my thoughts to places where my troubles seem so much further away and my joys feel like they're going to stay in my life forever.

I hope you'll stay forever, too. I feel like you're my soul mate. And I want you to know that my world is reassured by you, my tomorrows need to have you near, so many of my smiles depend on you,
        and my heart
                is so thankful
                        that you're here.

It would bring me more joy than I can say
if you would never forget
    — not even for a single day —
how wonderful you are...
        in my eyes and in my heart.

I'm so often at a loss to find the words
to tell you how much you mean to me.
In my imagination, I compare you with
things like the sunshine in my mornings,
the most beautiful flowers in the fields,
and the happiness I feel on the best days
of all.

You're like the answer to a special prayer.
    And I think God knew
        that my world needed
            someone exactly like you.

If I know what love is, it's because…
I know you. You are the reason for
so many of the smiles I have, and
you're the one place my heart always
wants to go — when it wants to feel
hopeful and grateful and glad.

If I know what love is, it's because my
thoughts of you have such a
beautiful way

of gently filling my soul…

My thoughts of you are my mornings'
inspiration and my evenings' comfort. They
are wondrous thoughts, free in spirit, and
they take me along when they're soaring
above the things that cloud other parts of
my life. You make everything all right in my
world, every time I think of you.

If I know what love is, it is because every
moment with you is a past, a present, and
a future that brings me closer to a wish
come true than any fantasy I've ever had.
With your own special magic, and in your
own marvelous ways, you have given my
days more richness and joy and love...

    than most people
       will ever dream of.

The things I promise to be for you

A place you can come to for comfort.
Eyes you can look at and trust.
A hand to reach out and clasp.
A heart that understands
     and doesn't judge.

A supportive shoulder to cry on.
A long walk anywhere you want to go.
And for any time when we're apart:
     a close and caring intimacy
          that you will *always* know.

A door that is always open. A caring,
gentle hug. A time that is devoted to
you alone.

     A reflection of my love.

The nicest feeling I've ever known
is being in love with you.

And I want to thank you
for these feelings...

For bringing me happiness
as though it were a gift
I could open every day
...I thank you.

For listening to all the words
I want to be able to say
...I appreciate you.

For letting me share the most
personal parts of your world
and for welcoming me with
your eyes
...I am grateful to you.

For being the wonderful, kind,
giving person you are
...I admire you.

For being the most beautiful
light in my life
...I desire you.

For being everything you are to me
and for doing it all so beautifully
...I love you.

Every time I say I love you...

I'm really trying to say
    so much more
    than just those three little words;
I'm trying to express so many
    wonderful feelings about you.

I'm trying to say that you
    mean more to me than
    anyone else in the world.

I'm trying to let you know that
    I adore you and that I cherish
    the time we spend together.

I'm trying to explain that
    I want you and that I need you
    and that I get lost
    in wonderful thoughts
    every time I think about you.

And each time I whisper
    "I love you,"
I'm trying to remind you
    that you're the nicest thing
      that has ever happened
        to me.

If I didn't have you, I don't know what I would do. For with you I have so much. Such sweetness. And happiness. And love.

You are a rare combination of so many special things. You bring me feelings that know no limits, and smiles that never go away. You are a part of every day of my life, whether you are close enough to touch or out of reach to all but my hopes and my dreams.

In everything, it seems like my life was just waiting for you. And with you here, I want you to know that I have never been so happy...

I love you for understanding me the way you do. And for caring. You have created lasting changes in my life and in the way I want tomorrow to be.

You have given me the courage to express what I feel inside. We have shared thoughts that have brought us together and that will keep us there from now until the end of time.

Our love is a gift that will forever be.

Thank you, sweet soul mate, for being mine. And thank you... for loving me.

Will Love Last?

One of the most valuable lessons
we can learn from life is this:

That, try as we might, we will never have
all the answers. We can wonder for the rest
of our days whether we are doing the right
thing... continuing in the best relationship
and following the best paths toward tomorrow,
but no one is ever going to answer those
questions for us.

We both may have wonderings of what to
do and curiosities of what's to come. Time
will help us with the results, but more than
any one thing, it's up to us — and to the
love we have for each other — to go in the
right direction.

You and I might sometimes wonder about
where we're headed and whether our love
will last a lifetime through. We may not know
the answer, but I'll tell you the one thing
I do know:

There's no one
I'd rather try to spend
forever with... than you.

Love Endures

There are few miracles in this universe as amazing as love. When it is true and real and lasting, it forms an unbreakable bond between two very fortunate people. It lets one know that it is always there, always caring. It lives in the deepest part of the heart, but it sneaks out as often as it can... to inspire a grin on the face, a smile in the eyes, a serenity in the soul, and a quiet gratitude in the days...

Love is giving and forgiving, taking and partaking of the sweetest joys and most comforting reassurances imaginable.

Love can work wonders. It can travel a thousand miles in the span of one second, and it can take every hope and well-wishing along with it on the journey. Love can feel at home no matter where it is, as long as it knows that it has a companion there by its side to make each place, each day, and each moment a space and a time of sharing.

Love is amazing, precious, and beautiful. It's there for the giving; here for the receiving. Love is what I want to give to you and what I pray that you will always share with me.

Love endures, and love will make sure
that we're as happy
as two people can be.

What do I want in a relationship?

I want emotional closeness.
I want sharing.
I want a beautiful bridge
    between us that is always there, always
    open, always secure, always ours alone.

I want communication.
I want words that speak our language.
I want touches that say more than
    words can mean.
I want to talk things over, whether they're
    little or large.
I want to be more in touch with you than
    I've ever been before...

I want the things we do to turn into some
    of the nicest memories any
    two people could ever ask for.

I want friendship. I want love.
I want gentleness. I want strength.
I want as much happiness as tomorrow
    can promise to anyone.

I want to be home to you.
    I want you to be home to me.

And I want the smile that is in my heart
    to always reflect so beautifully
    in the eyes I most love to see.

I found what I was searching for.
    And now, the thing I most want to do
    is to let you know
        how very much... I love you.

"One Thing Will Never Change"

Life is so unpredictable. Changes always come along... in big ways and small steps, sometimes giving us a little nudge and other times turning our whole world upside down. So many changes; some subtle and almost unnoticeable, some drastic and more difficult to deal with.

But throughout all of life's changing and rearranging, I'm so glad that there is one wonderful thing that will never change...

In the passing of life's moments, I
know that yesterday is already gone
and that tomorrow will soon be here.
The one thing I will take with me in all
of the days that lie ahead… is the one
thing that has seen me through so many
times in the past.

It's something that will never change.

You are such a steady, strong, and
beautiful part of my life. You never
cease to amaze me with the constancy
of your giving, the unselfishness of
your heart, and the reassurance of
your smile.

And I thought it would be nice to let
you know that you have touched my
very soul… and that my special feelings
for you
are going to last forever and ever.

Do you know how important you are to me?

I know you probably wonder
from time to time
what you mean to me.

So I'd like to share this thought
with you, to tell you
that you mean
the world to me...

Think of something you
couldn't live without
...and multiply it by a hundred.

Think of what happiness means to you
...and add it to the feelings you get
on the best days you've ever had.

Add up all your best feelings
and take away all the rest...
and what you're left with is
exactly how I feel about you.

You matter more to me
than you can imagine
and much more than
I'll ever be able to explain.

I care about you so much.

And that caring and that feeling
have a meaning that is more precious
and more special to me than
        words can begin to describe.

But let me try to tell you this...

Saying "I care" means that I will always
    do everything I can to understand.

It means that I will never hurt you.
It means that you can trust me...

It means that you can tell me
    what's wrong.
It means that I will try to fix what I can,
that I will listen
when you need me to hear, and that
— even in your most difficult moment —
    all you have to do is say the word,
        and your hand
            and my hand
        will not be apart.

It means that whenever you speak to me,
whether words are spoken through a smile
    or through a tear...
        I will listen with my heart.

I don't know exactly what it is... but there is something very special about you.

It might be all the things I see on the surface, things that everyone notices and admires about you. Qualities and capabilities. Your wonderful smile, obviously connected to a warm and loving heart. It might be all the things that set you apart from everyone else.

Maybe it's the big things: The way you never hesitate to go a million miles out of your way to do what's right. The way your todays help set the stage for so many beautiful tomorrows. Or maybe it's the little things: Words shared heart to heart. An unspoken understanding. Sharing seasons...

Making some very wonderful memories.
The joys of two people just being on the
same page in each other's history.

If I could ever figure out all the magic that
makes you so special, I'd probably find out
that it's a combination of all these things —
blended together with the best this world
has to offer: Friendship and love, dreams
come true, strong feelings, gentle talks,
listening, laughing, and simply knowing
someone whose light shines more brightly
than any star.

You really are amazing.

And I feel very lucky to have been given
the gift of knowing
how special
you are.

One of a Thousand Reasons Why You're So Important to Me

I love the fact that I can just be myself with you. That's something that seems to be so difficult with other people I know, and yet it is so natural and easy with you.

It's hard to explain how much that means to me, but trust me: it is absolutely invaluable. It means that you and I have a special connection that is bridged with complete honesty and trust. When I'm with you, I don't have to put all my feelings through a filtering process before I share them. You let me speak my mind and say what's in my heart without my having to worry about what you'll think if I say the wrong thing...

And even better than that... is the fact that
this understanding is a two-way street. You
can be just as spontaneous and as open with
me, and you know that I would never do
anything to alter that special flow of joy
and warmth and trust that goes between us.

I have a feeling... that once in a great while,
one person comes across another person
who is the perfect companion to walk with on
our travels through life. One of the reasons
you will always be so important to me is that

I love walking the way through
the journey of my days...
with someone as special as you.

Inside of me there is a place...
where my sweetest dreams reside;
where my highest hopes are kept alive;
where my deepest feelings are felt;
and where my favorite memories are
    tucked away, safe and warm.

My heart is a lasting source of happiness.
Only the most special things in my world
get to come inside and stay there forever.

And every time I get in touch with the
hopes, feelings, and memories in my heart,
    I realize how deeply
            my life
        has been touched by you.

A Little Love Story

When I first knew you, the thought of having you in my life was one of the most wonderful things I could imagine.

To have gone from that moment in time to this moment when I'm happier than I ever thought any person could ever be, is all the proof I'll ever need... to know that miracles really do come true.

This is my love story...
about you.

I love you. So much. And so amazingly. Each day is like a new page that I get the privilege of turning over, with a new paragraph for the morning, a sweet entry for the afternoon, and a can't-wait-to-read romance that winds its way to the brightest stars anyone ever wished upon...

Ours is a story of two people, each with
a journey in search of a distant horizon.
Two souls whose paths were allowed to
cross, whose words felt right at home, and
whose smiles discovered that walking the way
together could lead to a kind of happiness
that only comes along once in a lifetime.

We were given a gift that many people search
all their lives for and never manage to find.
When I found you, I just knew how I wanted
to fill the empty pages of my life.

I want to be with you... and I want this love
story to have a very happy ending...
by never, ever ending at all.

What Is Love?

Love is a wonderful gift. It's a present so precious words can barely begin to describe it. Love is a feeling, the deepest and sweetest of all. It's incredibly strong and amazingly gentle at the very same time. It is a blessing that should be counted every day. It is nourishment for the soul. It is devotion, constantly letting each person know how supportive its certainty can be. Love is a heart filled with affection for the most important person in your life. Love is looking at the special someone who makes your world go around and absolutely loving what you see.

Love gives meaning to one's world and magic
to a million hopes and dreams. It makes the
morning shine more brightly and each season
seem like it's the nicest one anyone ever had.

Love is an invaluable bond that enriches every
good thing in life. It gives each hug a tenderness,
each heart a happiness, each spirit a steady lift.

Love is an invisible connection that is exquisitely
felt by those who know the joy,
        feel the warmth, share the sweetness,
                and celebrate the gift.

There are many blessings to count in this world; good things and special people who keep smiles in the heart and joy in the days.

I have friends who are important to me. I have people I can talk to and trust. And relations whose common bonds will always be interwoven with love and togetherness.

But as radiant and as wondrous as even the very best people can be, no one will ever hold a candle to you.

Sometimes you feel like the answer to a prayer that I barely even got a chance to say. I was blessed with your presence from the beginning of our days, and the more time we spend together, the more clear the reason becomes to me...

I think that we have been given some of the
most beautiful presents this world has to give.
We have the joy and strength and support
of being true companions, and we have all
the feelings and special meanings that
treasure brings, all the "knowing why" and
the "understanding when." We have a sharing
instilled in us — and a kind of caring that
words can't describe. No matter how high
the walls may be between other people,
there is an open door between us that always
leads to love.

I think that God just knew that there would
be so many times when I'd need the blessing
of a soul mate like you.

And I lovingly keep discovering
          how precious that blessing is.

I receive so much joy from just being
able to see a smile in your eyes.
I love to look at you and realize how
incredibly glad I am for what we have
and everything the
                two of us share.

I need those moments in my life.
I need your goodness and your giving
        and all the memories we've made.
I need the promises and the plans
and the precious gift of simply
        holding your hand in mine.

It would be wonderful if all the wishes
I could ever imagine could find a way
to come true. But deep down inside,
I don't need all those wishes.

                All I need... is what I have
                        with you.

I want to thank you. So much.
I want to love you. With every
    smile and every touch.
I want to tell you how wonderful
    you are.
        I want to let you know...

You're my wish on every single star.

I want you to realize that you'll
    always be the only one who
    makes me feel like this.
And I hope you remember,
    long after this day is over,
    and far beyond each kiss...

In the "always" that lies ahead
and the "forever" that will be,

I'll still be loving you and thanking you
    for the joys you've given me.

There are a thousand things
I would like to be for you...
but one of the most important
is just being
    the someone
        you can talk to.

There are so many things
    I would like
        to do for you
and so many things I would like
to say and give and share.

But for today
    I just want you to know
that in addition to all the love
    I can possibly give,
I promise to be your friend
        for as long as I live.

I'll always be there,
        and I'll always care.

A Little Something for You...
to Read and Remember

I will care about how the world is treating
you every day of your life. I will wish
wonderful things for you. I will hope you
will be richly rewarded for all the joys you
bring to the days.

I will try to find a thousand ways of telling
you that you are so important to me. My
whole life long, I will remember every precious
thing about you.

I will think of the memories we have made
every time I need to shine some serenity
into my world...

I will smile whenever I try to count the
special blessings you've given me,
knowing that I couldn't count that high,
even if I had an eternity.

I will speak of you in glowing terms
whenever I tell other people about you.
I will realize that the bond I have with
you is one of the sweetest privileges of
my life. I will be grateful for the way
you've chased so many clouds away and
given my days such an abundance of
warmth and sunshine.

I will cherish you, care about you,
        and hold you close to my heart
        ...long enough to last a lifetime.

It would take me a lifetime to list
all the reasons why
you are so important to me.

It would take me forever to find words
for all the thanks I would like to express...
for all the deeply reassuring feelings I have
felt in your acceptance of me.

And it would take an eternity to
give you back even half
of the happiness you've given me
during the wonderful times we've shared...

But until forever is here,
until a lifetime is lived,
and until eternity gives me a chance
     to say everything
          my smiles try to show...

I will hold you in my heart
     more gently than any feeling,
I will keep you on my mind
     more lovingly than any thought, and
I will feel blessed by your presence
     more than you will *ever* know.

You are my own special miracle.

The days we share are my blessings.
The memories we make are my treasures.
The togetherness we have is
    my dream come true.
And the understanding we share is
    something I've never had
        with anyone but you.

If anyone ever asked me what part
of my life you are...
    I would just have to
    look at them and smile
    and say, "The *best* part."

The happiness you give to me is
something I'll never be able to get
enough of.

I love having you in my world.

And I love having you
    to love.

I want you to read this... today and
then again from time to time, just as
a reminder of how much I love you.

I want you to read this... so I can let
you know that the memories you have
given me are the most treasured things
in my life, and the love we share together
can't begin to be measured... by words
or even by smiles.

The feelings are far too valuable
        and the thoughts are so precious to me...

I want you to read this... because no
other feeling compares with the sweetness,
the warmth, and the wonder of you.
I could mention it to you every single day,
but I still couldn't say often enough how
much I love
         being together with you.

I want you to read this...
         because I want you
            to see for yourself
some of the things I quietly thank you for
when I get lost in my thoughts of you.

And I want you to read this... because I
always find that such an enormous part
of my happiness comes from sharing

         this dream come true.

I Will Always Love You

I am going to love you all of my life, through whatever comes along. The feelings I have will stay strong and true, knowing that our tomorrows hold so much promise for us.

I really think that you and I have an opportunity to be as happy as any two people could ever be. That's why this is what I would wish for, if I could
  have just one request…

Please…
  just keep on loving me.

Because no matter what comes along,
  if we just keep our love strong

      we can always
    work out all the rest.

I find that you're on my mind
more often than
    any other thought.
Sometimes I bring you there
    purposely... to console me
        or to warm me
        or just to make my day
        a little brighter.

So often you
surprise me, though,
and find your own way
    into my thoughts...

There are times when I awaken
and realize what
a tender part of my dreams
    you have been.

And on into the day,
whenever a peaceful moment
seems to come my way
and my imagination is
    free to run,
it takes me running
    into your arms
        and allows me
            to linger there...
knowing there's nothing I'd rather do.

I know that my thoughts are only
reflecting the loving hopes
    of my heart...
because whenever they wander,
    they always
        take me
            to you.

I love having you in my life. It has never been the same since you came into it, and I know it will never be the same again.

I love you so much. You are always inside of me, warm within my heart, and you are everywhere in the world that surrounds me. You come to me tenderly.

You take my soul places it's never been before. You give me more of you than I ever knew anyone could give.

You give me feelings that feel like presents almost too beautiful to open. Among the gifts you have given, one of the most wonderful of all is the joy of being so close to you. Thank you for trusting me enough to share all that you are... with all that I hope to be. I love catching glimpses of every new facet you share. And the more you do that, the more I can't help but adore what I see...

In the time that we have been together, you have made my sun rise on so many mornings — and I'm sure it was you who made my stars come out at night.

You've surprised me with the gifts of hope and laughter and love, and you've made me a believer in something I never used to have too much faith in: the notion that dreams really can come true.

If there are times when you look at me and see my eyes filled with smiles and tears, it's only because my heart is so full of happiness and because

my life is so thankful for
... you.